Odell Beckham Jr.

By K.C. Kelley

Consultant: Craig Ellenport,
Former Senior Editor, NFL.com

BEARPORT
PUBLISHING

New York, New York

Credits

Cover and Title Page, © AP Photo/Ben Liebenberg; 4, © Rich Kane/Icon Sportswire/Newscom; 5, © Max Faulkner/TNS/Newscom; 6, © AP Photo/Kathy Willens; 7, © AP Photo/Julio Cortez; 8, © Liquidanbar/Dreamstime; 9, © Rich Graessle/Icon SMI CGV/Newscom; 10, © Jonathan Bachman/Cal Sport Media/Newscom; 11, © John Albright/Icon SMI/Newscom; 12, © Tyler Kaufman/Icon SMI/Newscom; 13, © Matthew Visinsky/Icon SMI/Newscom; 14, © AP Photo; 15, © Tyler Kaufman/Icon SMI/Newscom; 16, © Rich Graessle/Icon SMI CGV/Newscom; 17, © Vinny Carchietta/ZUMA Press/Newscom; 18, © Pro Football Hall of Fame; 19, © Vinny Carchietta/ZUMA Press/Newscom; 20, © Art Foxall/UPI/Newscom; 21, © Rich Kane/Sportswire 781/Newscom; 22, © Rich Kane/Icon Sportswire/Newscom.

Publisher: Kenn Goin
Editor: Jessica Rudolph
Creative Director: Spencer Brinker
Photo Researcher and Production: Shoreline Publishing Group

Library of Congress Cataloging-in-Publication Data

Names: Kelley, K. C.
Title: Odell Beckham Jr. / by K.C. Kelley.
Description: New York : Bearport Publishing Company, Inc., [2016] | Series:
    Football Stars Up Close | Includes bibliographical references, webography
    and index.
Identifiers: LCCN 2015039499| ISBN 9781943553389 (library binding) | ISBN
    1943553386 (library binding)
Subjects: LCSH: Beckham, Odell, Jr., 1992—Juvenile literature. | Football
    players—United States—Biography—Juvenile literature.
Classification: LCC GV939.B424 K45 2016 | DDC 796.332092—dc23
LC record available at http://lccn.loc.gov/2015039499

For more information, write to Bearport Publishing Company, Inc., 45 West 21st Street, Suite 3B, New York, New York 10010. Printed in the United States of America.

10 9 8 7 6 5 4 3 2 1

Contents

Is Odell Ready?

Heading into the 2014 season, fans of the New York Giants thought **rookie** Odell Beckham Jr. was going to be special. The **wide receiver** was fast and could make almost any catch. However, he was unable to play in the first few games because of an injury. Many people wondered, what can he really do?

Soon after his injury healed, Odell finally had a chance to shine in a game against the Dallas Cowboys. In the second quarter, Giants **quarterback** Eli Manning threw the ball toward Odell.

Odell runs down the field, waving to let Eli know he's open.

Odell (#13) makes a catch early in the game against Dallas.

Odell had injured his hamstring during a 2014 **preseason** practice. The hamstring is a large muscle in the back of the thigh.

'The Catch'

Cowboys defender Brandon Carr tried to tackle Odell as he ran down the field, but nothing could stop the wide receiver. As Eli's pass came down toward Odell, he leaped backward. Then he reached out with his right hand . . . and caught the ball with just three fingers. Odell fell into the end zone—**touchdown**! His amazing one-handed catch had everyone talking. Many people called it the greatest catch they had ever seen!

Odell's teammates congratulate him after his unbelievable catch.

Odell reaches behind his head while he leaps to make the catch.

On Twitter, more than 23,000 tweets about Odell's catch were sent every minute in the hour following the play.

Childhood Dream

Odell Beckham Jr. was born on November 5, 1992, in Baton Rouge. His father was a football player at Louisiana State University (LSU). His mother was a runner on the school's track team. As a child, Odell spent lots of time playing football and running on the LSU **campus**.

When he was four, Odell's mother asked him what he wanted to be when he grew up. Odell quickly said, "I want to play in the NFL!"

The LSU football field

Odell with his mother in 2014

Odell's mother, Heather, won six national college championships as a runner. She later worked as a track coach for several universities.

Odell went to Isidore Newman High School in New Orleans. On the football team, he was a star wide receiver. Because of his speed, he was great at returning **kickoffs** as well.

As a senior, Odell caught 19 touchdown passes. He also scored six **rushing** touchdowns and scored two more on **punt** returns. Colleges all over the country wanted Odell to play football for them. He decided to stay in Louisiana and go to LSU.

Odell playing for the LSU Tigers

In high school, Odell played on an all-star team organized by the U.S. Army.

Odell was only the second receiver at Isidore Newman High School to gain more than 1,000 yards (914 m) in a season. The first was Cooper Manning, the brother of NFL quarterbacks Peyton and Eli Manning.

Right at Home

In his first year at LSU, Odell became a **starting** wide receiver. The Tigers' coaches helped Odell develop "great hands." That's when a player has outstanding catching ability. Odell was able to get downfield quickly and catch just about any pass. He also returned punts and kickoffs. Odell even ran back two punts for touchdowns in his second season.

Odell's speed has always made him hard to tackle.

Seven of Odell's touchdown catches at LSU were for 50 yards (46 m) or longer!

All-American

In his third season at LSU, Odell was named an **All-American** as a kick returner. He also set an LSU record with 2,315 all-purpose yards (2,117 m)—the combined total he gained as a receiver, runner, and returner. Odell **averaged** 178.1 all-purpose yards (163 m) per game. That was the second-best of any college player in the country!

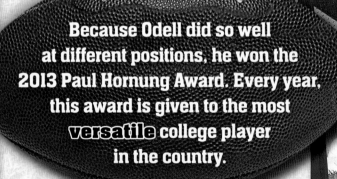

Because Odell did so well at different positions, he won the 2013 Paul Hornung Award. Every year, this award is given to the most **versatile** college player in the country.

NFL star Paul Hornung played for the Green Bay Packers in the 1950s and 1960s.

Odell was making amazing
catches even in his college days!

The Newest Giant

In the 2014 NFL **Draft**, Odell's childhood dream came true. The New York Giants chose him in the first round! Odell was eager to get started. Unfortunately, he injured his leg during a training camp practice. He had to watch the Giants' first four games of the season from the **sidelines**.

By October 2014, Odell was healthy enough to play in his first NFL game. He quickly made his mark and caught a game-winning touchdown!

Odell at training camp

Odell catches a touchdown in his first NFL game, against the Atlanta Falcons.

At training camp, NFL players get together six weeks before the season to practice with their teammates. The Giants' training camp is in New Jersey.

Beyond "The Catch"

The rest of Odell's rookie season was remarkable. He caught pass after pass and scored key touchdowns. Then came his one-handed grab against the Cowboys. Suddenly, everyone was talking about Odell. He could do more than just make one great catch, though. In the final game of his rookie season, Odell caught 10 passes for 185 yards (169 m), his highest total yet.

The Pro Football Hall of Fame in Canton, Ohio, has a display that shows the jersey Odell wore when he made the famous one-handed catch during the Cowboys game.

BECKHAM JR.
13

Odell catches a pass during the Giants' last game of the 2014 season, against the Philadephia Eagles.

Record-Setting Season

Odell had one of the best rookie seasons in NFL history. In 12 games, he caught 91 passes for 1,305 yards (1,193 m). In fact, he was the first NFL player ever to top 1,000 yards (914 m) after missing the first four games of a season. It was no surprise when Odell was named the NFL Offensive Rookie of the Year. With his incredible talent, Odell can expect to earn many more awards in the years to come!

Odell was named to the 2015 Pro Bowl. This is the NFL's postseason all-star game.

Odell sometimes likes to point toward the end zone after he makes a catch.

Odell's Life and Career

★ **November 5, 1992**   Odell is born in Baton Rouge, Louisiana.

★ **2010**   As a high school senior, Odell catches 19 touchdowns.

★ **2011**   Odell starts his freshman year at LSU.

★ **2012**   Odell leads LSU with 713 receiving yards (652 m).

★ **2013**   Odell is named an All-American kick returner.

★ **2014**   Odell is chosen by the New York Giants in the first round of the NFL Draft.

★ **2014**   Odell's amazing one-handed touchdown catch makes him a national star.

★ **2015**   Odell is named the NFL Offensive Rookie of the Year.

★ **2015**   Odell plays in the Pro Bowl.

Glossary

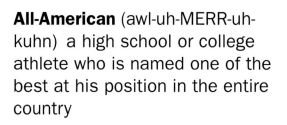

All-American (awl-uh-MERR-uh-kuhn) a high school or college athlete who is named one of the best at his position in the entire country

averaged (AV-ur-ijd) totaled about the same over a series of games

campus (KAM-puhss) the land and building or buildings that make up a school

draft (DRAFT) an annual event during which NFL teams choose college players

kickoffs (KIHK-awfss) plays made after a score or at the start of each half during which a team kicks the ball from the ground to the other team

preseason (pree-SEE-zuhn) the six-week period before the regular NFL season during which teams gather to train and play practice games

punt (PUNT) a play in which a team kicks the ball to the other team on a fourth down

quarterback (KWOR-tur-bak) a key player on offense for a football team who makes passes and hands the ball to teammates

rookie (RUK-ee) a player in his or her first year of a pro sport

rushing (RUHSH-ing) running with the football

sidelines (SYDE-lynz) areas next to the football field where players stand during a game when they are not playing

starting (STAR-ting) referring to a player who plays at the beginning of a game

touchdown (TUTCH-doun) a play worth six points in which a team carries the ball into the end zone

versatile (VUR-suh-tuhl) able to do several different things well

wide receiver (WIDE rih-SEE-vur) a player whose job it is to catch passes

Index

Bibliography

Odell Beckham Interactive Timeline: www.giants.com/interstitial/beckham13.html

Official site of LSU: www.lsusports.net

Official site of the NFL: www.nfl.com

Read More

Kelley, K.C. *Football Superstars 2015.* New York: Scholastic (2015).

Scheff, Matt. *Superstars of the New York Giants (Pro Sports Superstars).* Mankato, MN: Amicus (2016).

Learn More Online

To learn more about Odell Beckham Jr., visit
www.bearportpublishing.com/FootballStarsUpClose